To Mitchell f

INSTANT INK
Little Prayers

By Mary Erickson
Illustrated by Kate Taylor

A Breakfast Prayer

Dear God, you are a wise Creator.

Thank you for the  that gives 

, for the  that lays  , for the  that makes 

.

Thank you for  to make 

, for 

to make  , for 

to make crunchy 

. You thought

of everything I need for a healthy breakfast.

At Play

Dear Loving God, I know you want me to be kind and play fair. I can take turns

on the and .

I can share my  and .

I can be honest when I roll the and move my game piece.

Help me treat others the way I want them to treat me.

Before I Sleep

When I am tucked into my
on clear nights,

I look out my  and see your
bright lights.

The silvery and the

twinkling North .

I smile as I think, what a great God you are!
I know while I sleep, you will watch over me.
That makes me feel safe—as safe as can be.

At Christmas Time

Dear Heavenly Father, thanks for the

who sang to the

and for the that showed

the way. Thanks for the

that shared

and stable with Jesus you sent

Christmas day. Help me remember the

story of Christmas, when I see the

on the top of my .

Help me remember the reason for

Christmas. You sent Jesus

to say you love me.

My Birthday

Mother baked a three-layered

and put colored in a row.

My friend wore a purple party

and brought a  tied with a bow.

I'm grateful for my birthday, God.

I'm happy and I wanted you to know.

Remembering Easter

Dear Jesus, when people think of Easter—

some see a fluffy white

with a  of candy or colored

. Others see shiny new

or a fancy .

But I know Easter is more than that.

When I think of Easter — I see a

thorny and a rugged

on a lonely where Jesus

died for me. I see white

in bloom beside an empty tomb and

hear an say,

"Jesus is living again." Dear Jesus,

thank you for living in my .

Forgive Me, God

Forgive me, God— when my speak

unkind words, when my take me

where I shouldn't go, when my

push and pinch others, when my

is full of anger. Help me today, in all I do

and say, to follow in the footsteps of Jesus.

How To Be Happy

Grandmother said she feels happy when

she knits a . I feel happy too

when I brush my or help set the

with and .

Thank you God, I discovered when I make

others happy, I am happy too.

The Lord Is My Shepherd

You are like a Lord.

A leads his to green

pastures. He guides his  safely

over passes. He protects

them from a robber or a .

I am like a . Thank you for my

daily and my cozy  .Thank

you for your gentle that guides

me and protects me from danger. Thank

you, Lord, for being my Good .

Pets Are Fun

Pets are so much fun, Dear God.

Did Jesus have one when he was a ?

Was it a cuddly  that slept on

his ? Or a quacking that

ate all his ? Or a , or a

, or a instead?

I have a that lies down and

plays dead.

Thank you for pets, Dear God.

Wonderful Rain

You cover the sky with gray

and send to water the  .

I like the . It makes the

green. It makes ripen

and bloom.

fills our  and

rivers. It makes where

I can splash in my or sail

my . Thank you for the

and your great love.

Our Great Creator

You are the great Creator. You made the

and and .

You made the in the sea,

the in the ,

and  that roam the earth.

And you made me. I love you, God.

I will praise you with my whole heart.